THE CHANGING COLORS
IN A SUNSET

This is a book about caring, and warmth, and sensitivity. It's about people, the living Earth, and the relationship between the two.

Derk Janssen has captured in poetic form the essence of the unique tapestry woven by the multi-faceted citizens in the Southwest.

Bruce Babbit
Governor of Arizona

In our hi-tech, fast-paced society of the 1980's, it has become increasingly more important to slow down, get "in touch", and take time to smell the roses. Derk Janssen's poetry does just that! The deep feeling message of hope for humanity comes through on every page. A wonderful panacea I highly recommend for a tired, aching spirit or just "a breather". This book would be appropriate for young and old. The depth and perception are reminiscent of Richard Bach's Jonathan Livingston Seagull. A definite reading must for the sensitive person interested in staying alive and keeping himself tuned in to his world and himself.

Julie Van Schoyk
Public School Teacher & Counselor

THE CHANGING COLORS
IN A SUNSET

C. Derk Janssen

CLARION'S CALL
PUBLISHING

Printed in the United States of America
Library of Congress Catalog Card Number: 86-71710
ISBN 0-9617176-0-2

Illustrations by Yvonne Massey
Front Cover Art by C. Derk Janssen
Back Cover Photo by Michael Gooch

Second Printing

Clarion's Call Publishing
225 Cory Ave., Prescott, AZ 86301

C   O   N   T   E   N   T   S

Acknowledgements

Thanks to Harold & Rosemary; Andy, Eric, and
Matt; Deno and Agnes; Henry and Hattie; Vicki
and Melissa; Francine; Lori the Lion; Joe
Zuccarello; Seal Beach, Tucson, Fort Dodge, and
Prescott; and thanks to Prescott College and its
wonderful people and special feeling. For inspira-
tion, for insight, for love, for sharing ... I tip my
hat and thank you one and all.

*This book is dedicated to my
daughter, Melissa*

Preface

The American Southwest today is powerful, raw, and undergoing massive change. It is unpredictable, it is growing, and at times it is volatile.

For the past two decades, it has seen the influx of millions of new people, bringing an incredible diversity, and its resulting excitement and chaos. Mobility and transition continue to dominate the area.

This is the story of one person's struggle to find roots and values in the midst of a turbulent time and place.

Chapter 1

CONFUSION AT FIRST LIGHT

Asleep For So Many Years

The room was lit with two lamps,
I was sitting,
Head down, held in hands,
Tough times,
Thinking, pondering, wondering,

Suddenly, there was a light,
Not the light already in the room,
And I was jarred from a deep sleep,
... I was awake.

Quiet Mountain & Lake

Trust your inner instincts,
Your inner feelings,
Listen to them,
Feel them,

They can get buried with so many unnecessary details
and imaginings,
So many rocks thrown on the surface of the lake,

So smooth the water,
make it like glass,
And listen to what is deep inside.

Fortunate

That exuberance,
That urgency you feel,
... cherish it, cherish it,

That's life beating,
Life beating with all its force,

You are so fortunate,
so lucky to feel it.

Layers

layers,
and layers,
and heaps of superficiality,

and then discontent,
and the search
for depth begins,

the search for
a crystal, penetrating,
deeper understanding,

of this
all-consuming,
passionate,
adventure.

To Really See

It's the human spark,
The unpredictable,
The creative and spontaneous,
The acts of special courage,

That take us to the clouds,
to the mountain tops,
That allow us to really see,
to really feel.

Chapter 2

REBIRTH

One Sparkle

Moods and flows and ups and downs,
Thoughts and feelings riding the crests of
waves, running from stars and oceans
and air currents and water,
The fragility of life, feeling flowing through
you,
Fighting, striving to stay alive and maintain
harmony,
The wonder of circles and cycles, and ins and outs,
The pulse of the ocean and your blood,
The sparkle in your eyes and the stars,
Knowing you've been here before, and knowing what's
going to happen,
Being with someone for a year one night,
And someone else for a night one year,
The moonlight's sparkling in the snow, on the
mountain, off the water, at sea,
And in your eyes right through me.

The Other Side

The linear, logical,
rational vision,
is only part of the picture,

To see only that
becomes too dry,
too cold, too one-dimensional,

emotion,
passion,
intuition,
sensitivity,
... the other side,

is needed to complete
the image.

Rebirth

Once upon a time a young boy was walking through the forest, and he came upon a small, curious looking little book. On the cover was a drawing of a tree, and the words of a little poem. The poem read:

Now is the time for the pendulum to swing back,
Back toward spirit and renaissance,

Now is the time to heal the wounds of dissection,
Let us become whole again, with our minds and our
hearts in their proper place,

Let us open, open and feel the living Earth and
all its forms,
Let us rejoice in the waking of the magic Spirit
that connects all living things in wondrous harmony.

The boy became interested. He opened the little book, and read the following story.

The waves rolled into the shore with rhythm and grace. The pulse of the living Earth is beating on the shore of this beach. The wind that carries the waves and the birds fills my lungs and brings me life.

There is a oneness to all. Things may appear to be separate, but that can be an illusion. This planet is one living creation. The Earth is our body.

Misuse of science and language have created little, separate boxes in our minds. Along with a loss of perspective and balance, this has produced confusion and alienation.

It has also produced a fragmented, lost society, in search of connecting bonds. People look everywhere, but many of the routes are sorely lacking.

Perhaps there is an answer in understanding that there is more to living than separate boxes, material things, and machines. By refusing to value the heart, the Spirit, intuition, and the other intangibles in life, we cut ourselves off from the real power and wisdom. We are like the tip of the iceberg that does not recognize what is below the surface.

We take a baby at birth who needs the warmth and touch of her mother, and instead put the child in an incubating machine. We disdain the rays of the sun, and in its place, build nuclear power plants. We ignore natural ways, and prefer our own production of thousands of chemicals and other poisonous substances which have since contaminated our water, our soil, our crops, and the air we breathe. Only seeing the immediate, we have ignored the long-lasting. Only seeing the parts, we seem blind to the whole.

We wander lost in a superficial world, and can't seem to find our way out. Greed and the misuse of science have grown too strong. We are starving for Spirit, but we're walking away from it. We have cut so many of our ties to the whole of life, in our attempts to profit materially and conquer Nature, that we can't see clearly.

Perhaps we need a quest, an adventure, a rebirth— and exploration in search of our hearts, our intuition, our humanness, and our oneness with Nature. Perhaps we need to rediscover that intangible force that creates life, guides life, and connects life.

If we could find the middle path. If we could find moderation, and let it guide us. If we could see the unity all around, and let the forces of Nature work together, instead of against each other — there may still be time.

When the boy had finished reading the little story, he set the book down at the base of the tree. As he was doing this, he felt some letters engraved in the back cover. He turned the book over, and read the following ending poem.

Don't live inside the walls of part of your mind,
And surround yourself with too many things,
For you and all about you will become separated.

Strive instead for a balance between your head,
your heart, your body, and your spirit,

For there are realms within your reach, and
experiencing them will connect you within yourself
and with all living things,

The ancient myths, other cultures, the arts,
music, your dreams, and your connection with Nature,

Together with the mind's eye, they will help turn
lines into circles, and make you whole — don't
forget them.

The boy did not understand all that he had read, but he felt strangely moved by the little book. He left it at the base of the tree, hoping that someone would find it who could understand.

Light

So much of the world today is filled with machines
and science and isolation,

There need to be times of wholeness,
of healing,
of connection,

There need to be times when the Spirit that
fills people and Nature is awakened,

And brings light to our lives again.

Like A Pendulum Son

How does the world work Dad?
. . . It works like a pendulum son,

It goes back and forth,
and back and forth,

There are extremes, but ultimately . . .
there is balance.

Chapter 3

OBSTACLES IN THE WAY

Calls on Us

The answers are not always clear,
The path is sometimes dark,
... but we must walk on anyway,
we must move ahead,
because Life calls on us to grow,

It calls on us to become all that we are,
And we must have courage and faith during
those times when there is fog and darkness,
... and we must still walk ahead.

Preparing the Soil

The times that seem so hard, so difficult,
so confusing, so painful,

May be the ones you look back on as
the fullest,

Because the pain and confusion cut deep,
Preparing the soil,

Allowing the richness and depth
of life to pour in,

So that happiness, sadness, conflict, insight,
... all were really felt,
... all were really experienced,

Moving you, transforming you,
Changing you,
into something new, something better.

Born

Tear me down,
Tear me apart,
And let me put the pieces
of my mind, or my body,
or my life back together,

And in this way,
I learn,
I become aware,
I appreciate,
I see in perspective,
... humility is born.

Piece by Piece

Like the morning dove,
who patiently,
day after day,
slowly builds her nest,

Who steadfastly and repeatedly
flies to the ground,
finds a piece of dried grass and
returns to the tree,
over and over again,

We must all hang in there,
and slowly, gradually,
piece by piece,
build our dreams.

Lessons

We are each other's teachers,
All of us have lessons to learn,
and lessons to teach,

Let us perceive the teacher and
pupil in each person.

A Reason

There is a reason
beyond the temporary,
beyond the immediate,

Have patience,
hang in there,
... you'll see it.

Building

All the hardships, the challenges, the
trials, the tests,
The growing, the gradual improvement,
You are building a pillar of strength
within you,
You are building an identity,
Something, someone, to lean on,
. . . you are building yourself.

Toward

From fragments,
From confusion,
From falling apart,

Toward connection,
Toward whole,
Toward the middle,

Sink into it,
like roots,
Let it embrace you,
Let it take you,

... toward healing.

Longer

You can build buildings with mortar and
steel, and cement and wood, and they'll
last for a while,

... but the things you build with honesty
and sincerity last much longer.

Deep Inside

Sharing,
It's so important,

What is deep in your heart,
What is deep in your mind,

To help others,
To help yourself,

Sharing,
It's opening and connecting,
It's a risk,
But the reward is often life itself.

Also

If a force,
Or a problem
Or a situation,
Has the power to break you,
It also has the power to make you.

We Become

In our lives,
we are given tougher and tougher
things to beat,

And in this way
we become strong,
we become wise.

Chapter 4

A QUIET, RESTFUL MOMENT

Off-White

Liquid, flowing,
restful,

A deep sleep,
branches moving in
a calm breeze,

The sun is melting into
a pool of deep, deep
orange,

And you have drifted
backwards, far within
yourself,

To a quiet monastery,
off-white and still.

Woven All Around

There is a joy of living,
its pace is a little slower
than much of the world today,

It's a calm,
listening and looking,
walking in the trees,
smiling, talking with someone,
Letting the greens and yellows
quiet and lift you,

Taking you to the
quietly woven peace
all around,
To the
perfectly orchestrated
beat of time.

Clearing

City,
concentrated, packaged,
quick, quick, quick,
moments bursting at the seams and
crushing into each other,
exhilaration,
and burn hot, burn out,

Country,
stretching, flowing,
thoughts without boundary,
time has drifted, melted, and
fallen off the back porch,
The heart beats slower,
The breaths are deeper,

... there is a clearing.

Water & Earth

Time to leave the words,
Time to come out from behind their protective
walls and shiny robes,
To come down from the loft,

Time to touch the ground,
And feel the water,
And be quiet,
And wait,

Time to settle,
and receive.

To Lao-Tzu & The Deep Forest

It is called the Way,
It is quiet,
    submissive, yielding,
It is like water,
and tends toward the valleys,
It is weak,
    but in its weakness,
    there is unparalleled strength,
It is not the way of
the ten thousand things,
It is not the way of division,
and the multitude,
It does not concentrate on
the temporary, the material,
It is the one,
It is the beginning and the end,
It is from whence everything came,
And it is the force, the image,
We see deep in our mind's eye,
And feel in our hearts,

It washes away illusion,
It is clarity,
... it is the Uncarved Block.

Deep Breath

It won't work if you try to rush it,
Things need time to grow,

It won't work if you try to rush it,
Things . . . need . . . time . . . to
. . . grow.

Hear

Put your ear gently to the earth,
Put your ear softly to your heart,
And listen real close,
You can hear the heavens,
... you can feel forever.

In Sound

What pictures come
from the music?
What feelings are
born in sound?

Taking you back,
back to smiles,
and times of happy,
times of youth and energy
and undivided clarity,

The music, the sounds,
filling in the colors
to the beat of time.

Moments

You know, there are so many precious things in life,
    so many precious, beautiful moments,

Moments that fill your heart with joy, and your eyes with
    tears,

Moments that make you love life,

Oh, of course there are ups and downs,

But these moments of peace and quiet,
    of beautiful peace and quiet,

When you can sink into the heart of loving warmth,

These . . . are good moments.

Just the Size

So ... you're building your own world,
Well, have patience,

It'll take a while to build a world,
... even one just the size of your dreams.

Center

Getting in touch,
with the force that connects us all,

With the intangible, the invisible,
that sparkles, moves, runs through our fingers,
and reflects in our eyes,

You can feel it,
You can hear it,
You can touch it,

At the center,
... at the balance point.

Tapestry For All

to strive and strive
and strive,

and fall, and get
back up again,

quietly, patiently,
everlasting,

up the mountain,
towards perfect blue,
towards perfect white.

Within Seed

the one,
the essence,
the quietude,

to fall back within,
to be embraced,
and to embrace,

to feel whole,
and to watch the world with
clean, fresh eyes.

A Calm Tingling

The silence of the desert is all around,
And a quiet warming feel,
A calm, tingling of colors
and electricity,

The desert ... hold me,
Let me run, let me grow,
Let me see the clean, stark lines
of our nature.

Quickly

These poems are photographs, are pictures,
I see in my mind,
If I don't write them down quickly, they
are gone, like the changing colors in a sunset.

Chapter 5

OPPOSITES ATTRACT

If

If you have a heart that can break,
If you can cry,
If you can reach out to people,
If you can feel,
Then . . . you are very, very lucky.

Of All

Those that appear hard and aloof,
Are oftentimes the most sensitive,
That outer shell needs to be strong because they can be
hurt so easily,

Their hands may be cold,
and their demeanor withdrawn,
But if you're able to get behind their walls, you may
find the warmest, most caring people of all.

Turn A Corner

The place,
the time,
you turn a corner,
you open a door,
to look up
and find beautiful eyes
connecting with yours,

A river of time,
a path to follow,
the driving force
all around
and inside.

Can You?

Can you believe in something that doesn't
make sense?
Can you regain that childhood wonderment?
That smile, that youth, that refreshing
attitude that makes the world new?

I hope so.

Magnetic

She'll be there,
and I'll go,
we'll play out this scenario of romance,
this game of hearts, wits, and moves,

calling, calling,
        magnetic,

mystery and romance,
        delicious.

Last Night

It was tempest and fury,
leaping and running,
tense and exploding,
It was breaking shackles and burning down walls,

It was madness and a full moon,
searching, penetrating,
fire eyes,
It was a longing and an aching in need,

It was passion and torrent,
    it was last night.

Constant Sea

The lines separating us began to erase,
From dream world to real world,
We moved as one,

Our blood, our emotions, our spirits joined,
On a constant sea of up and down,
In and out,
We yearned,
    and connected,
    and separated,

And played parts in something bigger
than us.

Your Smile

Out of the fog, out of the fog,
Out of the holes, the stumbling, the dead ends,

Into your eyes, into your heart,

And flying above it,

To a place, a very special place of love and peace and
your smile.

Transfusion

People rub off on one another,
If they get real close,
they may actually connect,

You can't see the lines of connection,
But you can feel them,
And you can feel the energy moving from one person
to the other,

Like a transfusion,
the people's energy moves back and forth,
trading places ... mixing together,

That's why it's important who you choose to get
close to,
Because soon—you may be sharing the energy
inside them.

The Colors in a Prism

Diversity is what makes this world interesting and
fascinating,
It might possibly be less stressful and less confusing
if it was all like you,
... but fortunately it's not,

We need all the parts, all the differences,
It takes everyone to make this huge, magnificent
planet go around,
All the different shades, sparkles, angles, and hues,
So much for us to understand, to learn, and to enjoy,

... In each person, there is a separate universe.

If

Scientists say their data shows that the moon has
no effect on us,

They also state that their dials and instruments
prove that low level radiation does no damage,

But data, and instruments, and dials inside a
laboratory often have very little to do with
real life,

If you are sensitive, and if life is more to you
than a laboratory and machines,

... then you are aware of hundreds of things that
scientists know nothing about.

Mountaintops

Yes, I'm drawn to the mystical,
Yes, I'm drawn to the romantic,

And that has been the source of my smiles
and my sorrows,

The origin of my insights and
my delusions,

The reason for my times spent in the darkest of
caverns,
And on the brightest, most exhilarating mountaintops.

The Center

Let's quantify,
Let's measure,
Let's put it in the computer,
And analyze, and analyze, and analyze,

Let's label and categorize,
and label and categorize,

And gather statistics and data,
And more statistics and data,

We'll objectify it and sterilize it,
We'll minimize the human, and maximize
the machine,

And after all that — of course we'll
know it,

... Sorry, after all that, I think we will
have missed most of it,
We'll have missed the center, the mystery,
the essence.

Wrath

It's not science per se that draws
my wrath,
Or some of its remarkable physical achievements,

It's the way
that slowly,
gradually,
our minds,
our perceptions,
... our beings,
are changed
by the limits of physical tangibility,

We are beginning to believe in
and to trust
only that which we can physically measure,
And if we do that,
We will have lost the beauty,
and the magic,
And we will have lost most
of life.

felt & expressed

People need loving,
They need warmth, and hugging,
They need to know people care,
They need love coming through eyes,
through holding, through touching,

People need support, they need togetherness,
. . . they need it felt and expressed.

Chapter 6

S.O.S. - NATURE'S CALLING

And The Open Sky

There is power,
There is strength,
There is healing,

In the rocks, in the water,
In the earth, in the sun and
the open sky,

There is oneness,
There is transcendence in
Nature,

Please don't surround yourself
with too much of man,
For you will lose the connecting threads
to the essences, and
to the wisdom
beyond the illusion.

The Sound & Feeling

Too much people,
Too much using
and building,

Too much filling up every
corner
And on top of everything,

Not enough left alone,
Not enough solitude,

Not enough of the sound
and the feeling of
Nature embracing her children.

A Choice

Nature,
interconnected,
People, whole,
Sharing, open,
Colors of green, yellow, red, and blue,
Sound of the wind, and birds,
Feeling of exhilaration ... life,

Money, greed,
"Science",
Dissected, labelled, categorized,
Alienated, apart, alone,
Colors of gray, cement, and steel,
Sound of machines,
Feeling of emptiness ... death.

Fight

You are not finite,
You are not separate,

You are connected,
You are infinite,
You are everything, and you are forever,

So be selfish,
Fight for the rivers, the streams, the meadows,
the forests, and the air,

Yes, fight for them,
For they're all part of you.

Awareness

We do *not* know how wonderful, how exquisitely perfect the natural world is,

We also do *not* know how much damage is done by all the supposedly harmless things produced by man,

... our awareness of each should grow.

It Is Time

In "rising" above Nature,
we have dropped below our potential,

We have lost touch with
the sacredness,
with the power,
and with the dignity of the earth,

We have lost touch with the
natural forces,
... and with ourselves,

It is time to re-establish our
connections with the natural world.

Ticking

There's smiles, and money,
and excitement,
all over America,

... but quietly, slowly,
insidiously,
right below the surface of the glitter and fun,
something bad is brewing,

... there's an environmental disaster on
its way,
the water is contaminated,
our food is poisoned,
nuclear waste is leaking,
this country is a time-bomb,

And if we don't defuse it soon,
it's going to explode.

The Original Scheme

How it was intended,
That's what I'm concerned about,
To keep intact all the parts of the original plan,

Have we already lost it?
Has some of it been irretrievably altered?

Radiation, chemicals, genetic engineering,
... have they altered the original scheme of things?

Can lovers look into each other's eyes, and feel a
full, straight, pure shot of chemistry?

Can a mother breast feed her baby and feel confident
that the milk isn't poisoned?

Does the sound of rain give you a sense of peace and
security, knowing that the plants and crops will be fed,
and the air freshened—or, is the acid in the water
causing you concern?

Can't we clean it up—can't some thought be moved
from this year's profit margin to the preservation of our
lifeblood, the earth?

Is that so difficult?

... I pray that it isn't.

Our Body

The earth is our body,
Our veins - the rivers,
Our lungs - the wind,

It is time to stop the few,
Who are killing the body
of so many.

Cold & Gray

Shadows on gray,
cold domes,
Barbed wire, and the feeling
this belongs on an alien, dead planet,

... the feeling is true, for
they call it nuclear power,
and the image is one of hi-tech,
safe, modern efficiency,

... but the truth behind the shiny image,
is that the radiation emitted from the plants,
the radiation to be buried in the ground,
the radiation to be transported across the country,

... is so dangerous and destructive,
that the real words to be connected with it are—
environmental destruction, genetic damage, cancer,
leukemia, suffering, ... and death.

Why?

Why the kind of thinking that says people stand apart
from the natural world?
That allows radioactive waste to be produced,
Hazardous chemicals to be dumped?

Why the inablility to see that all is one?
That all is connected, that delicate balance exists, and
that it is so important for that balance to be maintained!

Why the thinking that allows atomic weapons testing,
strip mining, nuclear power plants,
and the smelters of acid rain?

Why the misuse of science that has allowed all of life to
be dissected into pieces?
And the world to forget about all the connecting bonds,
And the well-being resulting from those connections?

Why the mind that only sees the parts and never the whole,
that only sees the short-term and never the long-lasting?

Why? Why?
Too many why's,
Too many unanswered questions,
But let's at least give praise and respect to those people
who see the whole, who see the balance, and who see
that it should be preserved and maintained.

Tinkering

The atom is the basic building block of all life,
Splitting the atom for any reason,
... food irradiation, nuclear energy, excessive
x-rays, atomic bombs,
is an act of destruction,

If it's not stopped soon,
it will mean the end of life as we know it,

It's the biological chain,
it's the genetic blueprints,
it's the mystery, the marvel,
the perfection of life we are tinkering with,
... and we must stop.

Reckless

Science has given us much power,
But we use it recklessly,

We have a lot of gadgets and
chemicals and weapons,
But in the process, we are
slowly destroying the fabric of life,

We better stop putting so much
energy into being smart about
science,
... and more into being wise about life.

Are One

Rape the land,
And tear it,
And pollute it,
And poison it,

And then wonder why children
and animals are born with defects,
And so many of our people are sick,

... we must begin to see that the
land and the people are one.

A New Army

A major war is approaching,
Battle lines are forming,
Casualty lists are coming in,
The destruction of the living planet is progressing
on all fronts,
Ecological balance has been severely disrupted everywhere,
Money and greed and ignorance are winning,

We need an army of ecologists,
We need a new value structure,
We need a new strategy for survival,
We need a clarion trumpet call to wake up the citizenry
of the world,

It is time to chart a new course,
It is time to place the value of the environment
and ecology high up on the priority list,
It is time to say that
poisoned water, poisoned food,
rising cancer rates, rising birth defects,
more and more endangered species, and a dying,
unhealthy planet ... have all gone too far,

It is time for a change,
Time to heed the call,
Please lend a hand,
We need everyone,
Or else the war will be lost,
And the winner won't be politics or religion,

We will have lost this shining, magnificent,
fragile, spinning ball in space ... to
too much greed, and not enough knowledge.

I Wonder

There is flexibility, there is give, there is
patience in Mother Nature,

She seems to be able teach and correct where man
goes wrong,
But I wonder how long she can,

... yes, I wonder how long she can.

Cooperation

Nature has its own timetable for every
person, for every living thing,

In each seed there is a clock,
In every embryo there is a path,

Cooperation with Nature is necessary
for life, growth, fulfillment.

Miraculous

That fragility,
That sensitivity,

toward Nature,
toward each other,

I hope we can learn to
show our love and respect for
the miraculous gift of life.

Our Eyes

Traditional cultures,
the Tao of the Chinese,
the Mother Earth of the Native Americans,
warmth, harmony, feeling,

We laugh,
we scoff,
how primitive we claim,

It can't be measured,
It can't be programmed,
It doesn't exist,

We look with our eyes,
but we don't see.

To Rush Ahead

We rush ahead to join
    the glitter of the electronic
    age,
    to join the world of technology,

We can't wait to leave
    the farms, and the earth,
    and the wind and the trees,

And then slowly,
    and then quickly,

The bonds connecting
    our lives,
    fragment and break.

Circle

We think that time is a line,
And all things are separate,

But time is a circle,
And all things are connected,

We think that our progress
should be measured
by how much division,
by how much technology,
by how much individual profit
we can generate,

But instead,
our advancement,
indeed,
our survival,
need
union,
and connection,
and healing.

For All Is One

For all is one,
Every explanation,
every story,
every secret unfolded,
... is an analogy for something else,

Every stream,
Every organism, large and small,
Every hill, every mountain,
Every star, and particle of dust,
... is all the same,

We come from the same place,
We're going to the same place,
All the roads are connected,
And everything you see, though seemingly
separate,
... is all one,

Different phases, different looks,
different seasons,
But all hands are joined,
We defeat ourself when we fight,
... for it is like one hand hitting the other.

Crossroads

This society, this world is approaching a fork in the road,
Down one path are many, many man-made things,
Too many man-made things that are out of balance,
out of tune with Nature, with living,

And yes, we pay dearly for this path,
We pay with too many broken lives,
We pay because this is a path of weakness and ignorance,
And the bill each month, each year, is that the quality
of life outside and inside of us gets worse,
We pay because there are huge profits in weakness and
ignorance,
The manufacturers produce and produce,
and their profits go up and up,
and the consumers keep buying and buying,
And all the while there is dumping and dumping
and dumping,
and no one seems to care whether it's toxic wastes,
or poisonous chemicals, or plutonium,
... no one cares until it's too late,

But there is another path,
It is closer to Nature,
It listens to her, it respects her, it heeds her warnings,
and obeys her laws,

This path is about solar energy,
It's about unrefined foods and herbs,
It's about less electrical appliances, and a little
more physical work,
It's about exercise and preventative medicine,
It's about working with Nature, not against her,

It's about not so many chemicals and herbicides and
insecticides,
And more gardens, and healthier fruits and vegetables,
It's a quieter, softer, more human way,
There's less electric music,
More acoustic music,
Less television and radio,
And more talking, reading, and walking,

It's rest, pure diet, and home,
Not just surgery, drugs, and hospitals,
It's less traffic lights, office lights, fluorescent lights,
And more sunlight, more candlelight, more firelight,
It's less fast, fast, fast, this minute, this hour, this
profit chart,
And more quiet, slower, slower, listen, look, feel and
appreciate,

It's less things, and more spirit,
It's less man, and more Nature,
There's more warmth, more feeling, more caring,
It's closer to the earth, it's closer to God,
It's life, instead of death,
... and I hope, I pray we choose it.

If We Need A Guide

If we decide to change direction,
And move towards more respect for,
and more oneness with Nature,

And if we need a guide ...
He is among us now,
He is barely alive though,

For we have kicked, shoved,
humiliated,
... and nearly killed him,

He can teach us so much about
our connection with the land,
He was here before us,
And took care of this land so well,
for so long,

... we call him the Indian,
but he is the original American.

Splinters Into One

So many splinters
So many pieces,

We need to reach out and heal,
We need to work together,
And work very hard,

To stem the tide of
chaos and destruction,

We need to regain the Garden
And Wholeness,
And the dignity and magic
of Life.

This we know. The earth does not
belong to man; man belongs to
    the earth. This we know.
All things are connected like the
blood which unites one family.
    All things are connected.
    Whatever befalls the earth
    befalls the sons of the earth.
Man did not weave the web of life;
    he is merely a strand in it.
    Whatever he does to the web,
        he does to himself.

- Chief Seattle

Chapter 7

WHERE NO ONE'S BEEN

Growing

Growing is leaving the known for the
unknown,
Walking down a dark road,
Using for light whatever strength and
wisdom you have gained from your
previous steps.

Even More Now

So much change,
Waves and waves of destruction and creation,

The times today are filled
with stress and confusion,

There is so much pressure on
everyone and everything,

We must stand together,
We must have faith,
We must trust and believe in,
and support each other,
... even more now.

Seeds

Some of us were made ... not to fit into the traditions of this culture,

... but to be the seeds for a new one.

Respect

We all respond to a different calling,
We are all given different guides and
different paths to follow,

We must be tolerant and respectful of
the unique calling of each person,

Every generation also has a calling,
Some to farm the land,
Some to build factories,
Some to fight a world war,
And some to fight for the environment,

Just because they are different
doesn't mean we can't understand
and respect each other,
... let's try.

Brand New

There has never been what you are going to become,
You are walking down a brand new road,
There are no past models for you to follow,

There has never been someone just like you,
And there has never been what you can be,

So walk down that road,
Look straight into the darkness when
it comes,
... and become something brand new.

Find A Place

The land is powerful,
it can change us,
Every place on earth has a different quality,
a different energy,
And it can move you,
it can transform you,

Find a place that is
compatible,
A place that will
invigorate,
A place that will
provide for your
roots and branches.

Inside Out

It all flows from the inside out,
There is an innate, all-powerful,
intangible blueprint
that guides all of life,

All earthly manifestations are
expressions of that force.

Whole

We are all given parts of the puzzle,
We are all given a piece of the pie,
... part of the knowledge of how the
world works,

And what we need to do is to compare
notes,
Is to cooperate,
Is to share our part with others,
And if enough bridges are built,
... we will have a Whole.

Options

There is order,
There is destiny,
There is a Plan,

But the Plan has options,
Our effort, our wisdom, our willingness
to grow,

Will determine whether our individual
lives, and the life of this planet,
... will be a "10", or a "2".

To Create

To create,
To flow,

Can you feel the music,
Can you hear the words,
See the images, the colors,
the lines, the shapes,

Find it,
Go with it,
That creative instinct,
That force that can connect you
with the source.

Sparkling

The plant moves and breathes and lives,
the leaves flourish,
then gradually die away,
fall off,
and are replaced by new ones,

That happens to us too,
So open up, relax, venture out,
Let some old fade away,
Let some new come sparkling to
the surface.

Roots & Flowers

To unlock the potential
of our mind, our body,
our spirit,

is a quest,
an adventure,
an exploration,

... that never ends.

Somehow, Somewhere

One way or another,
You have to pay for everything you get
in this life,

Every moment of happiness,
of harmony,
of contentment,

Must somehow, somewhere,
be paid for,

It's the law of compensation,
of equality,
of balance.

Finally

A thousand forces,
emotions, desires,
moving you this way and that,
pulling, pulling, trying to gain control,

But quietly move toward the center,
And allow all the sidetracks to
vanish into thin air,

Come home to yourself,
And see things
finally
as they are.

From Ten Thousand To One

Purify,
Purify,

Simplify,
Simplify,

And allow yourself to
move within the balance
of heaven and earth.

Boundaries

I know when it was great,
Somewhere deep within my memory,
I can feel the humanity, the drama,
the passion,
... the majesty of nature and people,

When our existence was not
dominated by cold, sterile technology,
When the boundaries of our
lives, our emotions, our dreams,

were not drawn by computer bits
and nuclear weapons,

not backwards,
not regressed,
but forward, with balance.

The Price

Ideals conceived in the mind,
Need to be given life in the real world,
Need to be exercised, to be practiced in reality,
Resistance, resistance, and more resistance — that's
what the ideals will meet,

But that's the price for ideals — they're expensive,
     but they're worth it,
They've got to be.

In Tune

A new way is coming,
A way that is more in tune with
the living earth,

A way that sees the whole instead
of just the parts,
A way that puts health and
harmony above manipulating
people and harming nature,

A way to put this
country,
and this planet
back in balance.

Chapter 8

ONE CIRCLE

Spilling Orange

The sun rose quietly,
Slowly peaking its head over the
hills,
And then,
full of freshness and life,

Began spilling orange and yellow
and purple
across the valley and into our
tent,

Such a warm, clear trumpet-call beginning
to the day.

To Listen

Messages from inside,
Internal voices and guides
will tell you which way to go,
what holes to fill,
what you need to become whole,

Develop them,
nurture them,
help them grow strong,
Listen.

The First

The first real treasure you have is you,
Your path, your uniqueness,
Your special gifts and talents,

Hone them, develop them, trust them,
Don't let the wrong relationship,
the wrong job, or a false image,
... take you away from yourself.

Innate

You are the seed,
And the environment is the soil,

The soil can influence the direction
and quality of growth,

But cannot alter the basic nature of
the seed.

Pictures

The images produced in your mind,
Felt by your heart,

From music,
from stories,
from human drama and from art,

These will keep you alive,
These will keep the fires of your
spirit burning.

Spin & Stir

It's power and energy
moving in a direction,
It will take you,
It will carry you,

But you need to spin it,
and stir it, and build it,

It takes effort,
but once you get it going,
It can carry you to the threshold
of your dreams,

So move that rock,
Get it rolling in a positive,
creative direction,
It can inspire a person, a town,
a country,
... it's worth trying
to get momentum
on your side.

Your Little Corner

Please don't underestimate your contribution,
Life needs you to secure your little corner of
the world,

It may seem small to you,
But all corners are important,
It takes success in many, many parts for the
Whole to work,

So stay with it, and take pride in that
little corner, that little space,
that you're able to create and secure.

The Contest

You are not in competition with
anyone else,
You are in competition with
yourself,

To see if you can actualize
who you are,
To see if you can reach your potential,

... that is the goal, that is the
contest,
that is what will bring satisfaction
and fulfillment.

Vulnerable

You are vulnerable,
You are needy,
You can be swayed,
... when you are not whole,

To be whole means to have developed
your mind, your heart, your spirit,
and your body,
To have developed them to the fullest
of your ability,
And to have welded them together into
one unified force.

Strong Enough

Getting in touch,
     is getting strong enough to listen to yourself,
     to believe in what you hear,
     ... and to do something about it.

Your Voice

You must stand up for yourself,
And *keep* standing up for yourself,

You must speak out for yourself,
And *keep* speaking out for yourself,

You must speak up for what you believe
to be true and fair and just,
You must keep speaking up,
... your voice must never be stilled.

Full

It's a spectacular world,
Full of mystery and challenge and
hardship and joy,

Live it, live it,
And please don't be afraid to
walk straight ahead into the
unknown.

Each Day

Each day you begin with a new easel,
Each day you begin with a new mound of clay,

Each day you get to *begin* again,
Each day you get to create,

Each day is a space of white in front of you,
Each day you get to fill in the colors.

Adventure

Life is magical,
Be open to it,

Have the courage
To live the adventure that is you.

Typesetting by Dona Tanttila
Lay-out and paste-up by Ramona Vogrig